The KEN VALLEY

by
Jack Hunter

This modest building stood just outside New Galloway on the Newton Stewart road: the dyke at the roadside can be seen in the left foreground. Since then it has had several changes of name and been completely rebuilt, now transformed into the handsome, wooden bungalow 'Cairnraws'. The choice of site was an inspired one: the house enjoys a stunning view far down Loch Ken.

C. H. Dick, author of *Highways and Byways in Galloway and Carrick*, said that it was difficult to write 'with brevity or sobriety' of the road from Laurieston to New Galloway. Woodhall Loch, just north of Laurieston, is one of its main attractions. The scenery is less fine than formerly, however, after the cutting down of the oaks and beeches planted by Mr Hutchison of Laurieston Hall and their replacement by Forestry Commission conifers. S. R. Crockett tells how as a child homeward bound from school on winter afternoons he passed the notorious bogle thorn, seen nearest the camera, with some apprehension. He was right to feel so: Galloway tradition sees thorn trees as belonging to the fairies – not harmless, ethereal denizens of the Christmas tree but malicious creatures, possessed of supernatural powers and frequently hostile to human beings.

ISBN 1 84033 161 5

FURTHER READING

In compiling this publication I have referred to many earlier works on the area, most of them long out of print. The main ones are listed below, while others are mentioned in the text. I am happy to acknowledge my indebtedness to all the authors whose books I have consulted. Please note that none of the following titles is available from Stenlake Publishing.

Dick, C. H., *Highways and Byways in Galloway and Carrick*
Donnachie, Ian, *The Industrial Archaeology of Galloway*
Gifford, John, *The Buildings of Scotland: Dumfries and Galloway*
Harper, Malcolm, *Rambles in Galloway*, second edition
M'Conchie, Wm., *Tours in Galloway*, 1907 and 1915 editions
M'Kerlie, P. H., *History of the Lands and their Owners in Galloway*
Maxwell, J. H., *Guide Book to the Stewartry of Kirkcudbright*, eighth edition
Pigot & Slater, *Commercial Directories of Dumfries and Galloway*
Smith, David L., *The Little Railways of South-West Scotland*
The Statistical Account of Scotland
The New Statistical Account of Scotland
The Third Statistical Account of Scotland

ACKNOWLEDGEMENTS

I have to thank the following people for information: Miss Callander, Parton; Mrs H. Davidson, Newton Stewart; Mr W. Kerr, Stranraer; Mrs and Mrs Muir, New Galloway. However, any factual errors and all opinions and conclusions are solely my responsibility.

INTRODUCTION

Any discussion of the waterways of the Ken valley runs into serious complexities of nomenclature. The change of name from River Ken to Loch Ken south of New Galloway is only mildly confusing; the real problem arises with the arrival of the Black Water of Dee into the loch at Boat of Rhone. Below this point three different names for the waterway are championed. Some writers continue to call it Loch Ken; others refer to it as Loch Dee; while a third body of opinion favours River Dee. The Ordnance Survey cravenly sits on the fence and offers 'Loch Ken or River Dee'. In the interests of simplicity I propose to call the entire stretch from New Galloway to Glenlochar Bridge and barrage Loch Ken. (A change of name at Glenlochar seems logical, for the barrage physically divides the waterway, although whether it is equally logical to call the river below Glenlochar the River Dee might perhaps be questioned. After all the Black Water of Dee is the tributary and the Ken the major source.)

The Glenlochar barrage was built as part of the hydroelectric scheme to create a reservoir for Tongland power station downstream, and by raising the level of Loch Ken by four feet substantially increased its size. However, the impact of the power scheme on the landscape south of New Galloway took the form of modification rather than transformation.

Even before this expansion of 'the great Loch of Kenne Water', local opinion seemed divided on its contribution to the valley scenery. Alexander Trotter of Dalshangan considered it 'the glory and boast of the upper section of Kirkcudbrightshire' whereas William Learmonth of Gatehouse described certainly its north end as 'no loch at all but merely the expansion of a sluggish river dreaming along between widespread, lonely banks'.

What is beyond dispute is the importance of Loch Ken in earlier times as an artery of north-south transport. When the Gordons of Kenmure owned Greenlaw, below Glenlochar, not only passengers but furniture frequently moved by water between there and Kenmure Castle, approximately eleven miles to the north. Commercial use was also made of the route. After Gordon of Culvennan had cut a canal to link Carlingwark Loch with the River Dee in 1765, cargoes of marl, an excellent natural fertiliser obtained as mud from the bottom of Carlingwark, were transported by water up to New Galloway to the great benefit of agriculture there. On the return journey the barges carried timber.

But something greater was planned for the Ken, as the Crossmichael minister enthusiastically reported in 1790. This was no less than a proposal to link it to the sea at Kirkcudbright by a navigable waterway, allowing vessels to reach Dalry with a possible extension all the way to Dalmellington in Ayrshire. A survey was carried out for a canal to run on the east side of the River Dee from Kirkcudbright through 10 locks to Glenlochar Bridge and Loch Ken. At the north end of Loch Ken a further stretch of canal would take the navigation to Dalry, a total distance of 26 miles at a cost of £33,000. A company was formed and the necessary bill passed in parliament, but at that point the promoters returned to the real world and the Glenkens canal never left the drawing board.

The Ken valley also provided a convenient route for land traffic with its drove roads, by which huge herds of local and Irish cattle were taken to the markets of south-east England. This trade peaked between 1790 and 1815, when 30,000 animals went south annually. New Galloway, on one of the main drove roads from Portpatrick to Dumfries and the south, was also a collecting centre or trysting place for Stewartry cattle joining the droves, hence its cattle market and tannery. From New Galloway one of the drove roads to Dumfries ran down the east side of the Ken by Shirmers and Parton before crossing the hills to Kilquhanity and Kirkpatrick Durham. Feeder roads ran up both sides of the loch to New Galloway, as Silver Sand explains in *The Raiders*.

These roads brought problems to the valley because they were unmade and unfenced, and marked only by the animals' feet. The passage of a herd brought noise, dislocation, and damage to crops. Attempts by local residents to obtain compensation from the drovers led to 'riots and bloodsheds' according to a Privy Council report. In the case of one luckless drover the journey also led to a supernatural encounter. While checking his herd during a night-time halt on the Parton to Kilquhanity stretch, he encountered the Headless Piper of Pattiesthorn, bathed in blue light, the victim of a murder many years before.

However, the presence of the drove roads allowed several local men to become involved in the droving trade as entrepreneurs: Hope of Glenlee, Campbell of Chapmanton, Murray of Troquhain, and M'William of Glenlaggan, among others.

The Ken valley facilitated north–south communication but presented a substantial obstacle to travel between east and west, particularly before the building of the Ken and Glenlochar bridges at its two extremities, the latter in the early nineteenth century. Until then travellers had to use fords and ferries, despite the fact that – in Crossmichael parish at least – the fords were said to be dangerous and the cause of several drownings. In addition to Boat of Rhone north of Parton, ferries operated at Boat of Balmaghie and Boat of Livingston further south.

The Gordons were the dominant family along the Ken for centuries. At their peak they could claim one peerage, two baronetcies, and around 30 members of the landed gentry. They secured their position by insisting that, when a Gordon lady married, her husband adopted her surname, receiving as compensation a boll of meal and other privileges. This gave rise to a traditional local insult: 'Ye're nocht but a bow o' meal Gordon'.

Despite these precautions, the family had virtually died out by 1900, as foretold in an old prophecy.

Gordons, ferries, and drove roads may all have long gone, but the magnificent scenery of the Ken valley still remains, a fitting context for its rich history and lore.

According to S. R. Crockett in *Raiderland*, this house, shoehorned between Loch Ken and the road from Mossdale to New Galloway, was known in the late nineteenth century as Snuffy Point. This, Crockett claimed, was because one of its occupants used so much snuff that the Ken was coloured a deep brown for half a mile out from the bank every time he sneezed.

The village of Laurieston grew up at this crossroads, where the east–west road from Glenlochar to Gatehouse intersects the north–south route from Ayr to Kirkcudbright. This picture shows the start of the Laurieston to Gatehouse section, a way of wild grandeur, which, tradition says, inspired Robert Burns to write *Scots Wha Hae* while traversing it in a thunderstorm. Where exactly he committed his composition to paper is a fertile source of local controversy. The scene is much changed today with several of the buildings demolished, including Mr Campbell's one-storey clothier's shop in the left foreground. This was the modest successor to four tailors' businesses which existed in the village in 1852. The last two-storey building on the right is now the Laurie Arms; previous Laurieston inns have borne such picturesque names as the Compass and Square and the Dolphin.

The view back up to the Head End of the village and the crossroads. Almost all the whitewashed houses fronting the street have gone, to be replaced by the two-storey local authority houses of Crockett View. The novelist S. R. Crockett expressed his views strongly on the village's change of name from the original Clachanpluck to Laurieston, accusing 'a certain name-changing fiend . . . probably some Laird Laurie with a bad education and a plentiful lack of taste' of the deed. The change was indeed made after the Lauries of Redcastle purchased the estate in the eighteenth century. The original Gaelic name means 'village of clods', a reference, we hastily add, to the nature of the soil.

The description in *The Raiders* of the village's 'whitewashed houses and trees growing about the little fringes of garden' seems appropriate. However, the bridge over the Camelon Lane in the foreground is a reminder that the availability of water-power led to industrial development in the nineteenth century, with both a sawmill and a bleachmill in the neighbourhood, served by a local millwright. Before the creation of Castle Douglas by Sir William Douglas in 1792, Laurieston was the biggest settlement in the central Stewartry, and as such had an administrative function, the presbytery of Kirkcudbright meeting here.

The shop on the right is one of four which traded in the village in its heyday. Laurieston's most celebrated shopkeepers were the three unmarried M'Haffie sisters, who jointly ran a grocery business in the late nineteenth century. Staunch adherents of the Reformed Presbyterian faith, they walked seven miles to Castle Douglas each Sunday to worship in their chosen church. The purchase of a quarter of tea could involve the customer in an hour's religious discourse. Another notable resident of a slightly earlier date was the schoolmaster, Dominie Hutchison, not only a gifted teacher but a skilled, if unqualified, doctor, whose medical services were much in demand. This view was taken before 1932 as in that year the S. R. Crockett memorial was erected on the hillock in the centre of the picture.

The site for the monument to Galloway's best known literary figure is an appropriate one, as it is less than three miles from his birthplace and in the heart of the area he made famous in his works. Abandoning poetry on the advice of R. L. Stevenson, Samuel Rutherford Crockett achieved instant and spectacular success as a novelist, writing mainly but not solely historical fiction. A prolific, arguably over-prolific, writer, he alternated Galloway-based books with others set in Europe. Too sentimental for contemporary taste, he was a first-class storyteller with a powerful imagination and a sure touch with the supernatural. His best works, set locally, include *The Raiders*, *The Grey Man*, and *Men of the Moss Hags*. His memorial was unveiled in June 1932 by his widow. The main speaker was Galloway's other literary giant, Sir Herbert Maxwell of Monreith, and one of the contributors to the memorial fund was the present Queen Mother, then the Duchess of York.

Crockett was born here, at Little Duchrae, in 1859. His mother, a single parent, was the daughter of the tenant farmer, William Crockett. The author-to-be first attended school at nearby Laurieston and later at Castle Douglas (the Cairn Edward of his books) when the extended family moved there. At seventeen he won a bursary to Edinburgh University, where he supplemented his meagre income by journalism and thus discovered his eventual vocation. After graduation he obtained several travelling tutorships, which took him all over Europe, gave him a taste for that continent, and allowed him to meet the famous German Chancellor Bismarck. A return to Edinburgh brought him a divinity degree and appointment as Free Church minister to Penicuik. Achieving instant success as a novelist (*The Raiders* almost sold out on publication day) he gave up the ministry to become a full-time writer in 1895. He made frequent visits to Galloway and the Continent from his home in Peebles, dying near Avignon in France in 1915.

Laurieston Hall has endured two changes of name: from the original Grennoch, to Woodhall, to its present appellation. The building itself has been through similar alterations. The oldest part, the tower on the right minus the top two floors, is recognisably a seventeenth century tower house. Several eighteenth and nineteenth century extensions produced the version seen here. After the last set of alterations a contemporary writer enthused that the house incorporated 'the latest lighting, sanitary, and other improvements'. When the estate was broken up in the early 1950s the house was bought by Stewartry County Council for use as an infectious diseases hospital, and it was later used by Dumfries and Galloway Hospital Board as an outstation of Lochmaben Sanatorium. No longer required for that purpose, it is now the home of a community of craft workers and artists.

Well off the west side of the road at the head of Woodhall Loch, Slogarie (left) is first mentioned in 1606, although the present house dates from the end of the nineteenth century. In earlier times it was notorious as the residence of the Laird o' Slagarie, 'one of the wildest wretches ever known in the world'. The Laird and his two bosom cronies perished after a night of excess at the home of one of them, Auchenhoul. Their carousing ended with the burning of a Bible, shortly after which a terrible storm arose, a nearby haystack was struck by lightning, and the wind-driven flames engulfed Auchenhoul. With the well inexplicably dry, the two cronies set out separately to summon assistance, only to die horribly in accidents. Meantime the Laird re-entered the burning building to retrieve his wallet and was trapped by a falling beam, perishing in the flames. Today Slogarie is the headquarters of the Angela Gore company, which designs and manufactures women's clothes for a mail-order niche market.

The mansion and estate of Hensol provide another example of a lost Gaelic place name, for both were formerly called Duchrae, the change to Hensol being made around 1860 by a proprietor wishing to perpetuate the name of a deceased friend. Predictably S. R. Crockett, born on the estate, was less than approving of the alteration. Like nearby Slogarie, the name of the estate first occurs around 1600, but the present house is of nineteenth century origin, having been built in Tudor style but of local granite in 1824. Duchrae or Hensol estate was the scene in 1724 of the last episode of the Levellers' rising, when their forces were scattered near the Duchrae wood by regular cavalry. The rising was almost the only instance in Scotland of dispossessed small tenant farmers taking direct action against the agricultural changes that had cost them their farms and livelihoods.

The Black Water of Dee marks the boundary between Balmaghie and Kells parishes, but this is still Crockett country as the caption on this postcard attests. The bridge is the scene of one of the most exciting episodes in *The Raiders*. Gypsies driving stolen cattle from the lowlands to their stronghold in the Galloway hills are halted here by the Maxwells and other lowland lairds determined to get their animals back. The plan works initially, but is defeated by the ingenuity and daring of the gypsies, who break the blockade and sweep on to the hills unhindered. In fact the bridge featured in the novel is not the one shown here but an earlier structure, whose remains are still to be seen a few yards downstream. It is claimed that pearls of good quality have been obtained from the Black Water.

Crockett's "Raiders" Bridge New Galloway Station

No trace remains of this former shepherd's cottage, which stood a short distance south of Mossdale (where New Galloway station was situated) on the east side of the road. Like the nearby bridge, Crockett used it for the setting of a scene in *The Raiders*. There it becomes the small farm of Mossdale, home of Sammle Tamson and his sharp-tongued but kindly wife, Eppie. The couple are two of the most attractive characters in the book, in which they play a modest but not insignificant role. Their connection with Patrick Heron, hero of the novel, begins when he retires to their dwelling to lick his wounds after the battle at the bridge. Eppie's description of her husband as a 'great moidered knowt' is a reminder of the author's mastery of the Galloway dialect.

MOSSDALE, KIRKCUDBRIGHTSHIRE

The clachan of Mossdale (also known as Bennan, and the former location of New Galloway station) has an unusual street plan. Whereas most villages show ribbon development along the road, Mossdale lies at right angles to it, but parallel to the railway. This raises the possibility that most of the clachan was built after the construction of the Castle Douglas to Stranraer line between 1858 and 1861. Certainly an encampment of huts to accommodate the navvies building the line was located at Mossdale. In the foreground the road rises to the railway bridge. The hill in the right background is Bennan, from which, tradition says, cannon balls were quarried to be fired by Mons Meg at the siege of Threave Castle.

New Galloway station features in John Buchan's *The Thirty-nine Steps* as one of those used by Richard Hannay in an attempt to shake off his pursuers during his brief visit to Galloway. The New Galloway to Laurieston road originally crossed the line here by a level crossing; the bridge in the centre of the picture was built following an accident in November 1861, shortly after the line opened. The station was the scene of another accident in October 1913, when the fish train from Stranraer, travelling too fast, was derailed, scattering barrels of fish over a wide area.

New Galloway Station.

A wonderful range of vehicles waits to take passengers arriving at New Galloway station to their destinations. In addition to the regular bus or coach service, individual hotels provided their own transport to and from the station. These transfers (to use the parlance of the modern travel agent) were required because the station was over five miles from the town of New Galloway. However, in this respect the burgh was no worse served than Gatehouse and Creetown farther west; indeed the distance between town and station was even greater at the former. The reason for this inconvenient situation was that the railway was primarily built to link the national rail network with Northern Ireland via the Stranraer ferry, and took the shortest route across Galloway to achieve this. Local traffic was not a major concern. This fact was also reflected in the timetable.

Between Mossdale and New Galloway the close proximity of road to loch makes this an appealing stretch of shoreline for anglers in pursuit of perch, pike, and trout. The distance between water and road became even smaller after the hydroelectric scheme raised the loch level above that shown here. It would be a happy, if unlikely, coincidence if the motor vehicle was one of the Galloway range built a few miles downstream at Tongland in the 1920s by the Galloway Engineering Co. Ltd., a subsidiary of Arrol–Johnston. The Galloway range did include a four-seater, costing £350 in 1923, but the beautifully restored Galloway car in the Museum of Transport in Glasgow is the two-seater version.

Strategically situated to command Loch Ken and its valley, Kenmure Castle was for long the main residence of the Gordons, the most famous of the old Glenkens families. They came to the Stewartry from the Borders in 1440, and their surname derives from the parish of Gordon there, imaginative local accounts of its origin notwithstanding. Known originally as the Gordons of Lochinvar because of their ownership of that estate, they may in fact always have lived at Kenmure. Their two outstanding features were their loyalty to the Presbyterian cause and, somewhat contradictorily, to the House of Stuart. The former brought them the friendship of the famous minister Samuel Rutherford and expulsion from their castle by Claverhouse. The latter earned them a viscountcy from Charles I and cost the 6th Viscount his head for his support of the Old Pretender in the 1715 rebellion. The direct line ceased in 1847.

As can be seen here, Kenmure Castle dates from several different periods. The original castle, on a natural mound, may have been built by the Lords of Galloway but the earliest part of the present building only dates back to the sixteenth century. 'The great attraction and boast' of the area, it sufficiently impressed Burns when he visited for him to plan verses in its praise, but these did not materialise. The numerous alterations, extensions and demolitions are not surprising since it was burned by the Regent Moray and besieged by Oliver Cromwell's troops. Badly damaged by fire around 1950 and converted to a hotel in the 1960s, it is today roofless and derelict. Like Robert Burns, Mary, Queen of Scots, also slept here.

A. 2141.　　　　　　　　　　　　　　　New Galloway.

From the high ground to the south-west the street plan of New Galloway is clear: the main street is situated on the Kirkcudbright to Ayr road as it snakes along the west slope of the valley, and short side streets run off to the left and right. Scotland's smallest royal burgh dates from the seventeenth century. In 1629 Sir John Gordon of Lochinvar obtained a charter from Charles I to erect a royal burgh on his land. The intended site was near Dalry, but the plan was altered and the following year Gordon obtained another charter to create his royal burgh at the clachan of Roddins or Roddings of Ballingait, close to his residence, Kenmure Castle. The council of the new burgh was to consist of a provost, four bailies, and an ambitious twelve councillors.

At the south end of New Galloway the eye is caught by the bow-ended building on the right, which looks like a toll house. In fact it is one of a pair of buildings guarding the entrance to Meadowbank house. Just behind the photographer, on the right, grassy terraces in a steeply sloping field may be connected with the earlier settlement of Roddings. The snowy scene brings to mind an old tale of a heavy snowfall, after which the burgh's main street was buried in snow with the only sign of its existence being smoke coming out of holes from the chimneys of the single-storey houses. If the tale is to be believed, the residents dug tunnels from house to house to permit communication.

Set well back from the street behind its unusual entrance, Meadowbank was built in the early nineteenth century to look down Loch Ken. The house has links with two prominent local families. At the start of the nineteenth century it was the home of the Murrays, the head of whom was provost of New Galloway as well as a farmer and expert livestock valuer. Genial, witty and convivial, Provost Murray was a leading member of the community. His son George, the 'poet priest of Balmaclellan', achieved similar local eminence. Later in the nineteenth century Meadowbank effectively became the dower house for the Kenmure estate as the home of the Dowager Viscountess of Kenmure. From 1962 until 1974 it was a private hotel serving legendary afternoon teas.

Contrary to the air of well-being apparent here, the infant royal burgh got off to a bad start, its founder dying before his plans for the development of Galloway or New Town of Galloway could be completed. According to an unsympathetic local writer, after 150 years it was still so little developed that its only two-storey house was the 'whuskey-shop', and to fill the top council posts servants had to be drafted in from the castle. Even local man Robert Heron conceded in 1793 that the houses were 'low, ill-built, [and] thatched with straw', and a government report of 1832 condemned it as a poor place without trade or manufactures. However, as early as the 1680s it had a good weekly market, particularly for meal, and only twelve years after the government report the parish minister could record a changed picture, with a branch of the Edinburgh and Glasgow Bank established, the market for cattle thriving, great improvements in the houses of the residents, and a general sense of progress.

The focal point of New Galloway, where the old Edinburgh to Whithorn road crosses the High Street. In the right foreground the town hall, with the jougs, former implements of punishment, hung menacingly above the door. Beyond, across the modern Duke Street, the Kenmure Arms. To the left, at the corner of High Street and the West Port, lies Alexandra House, premises of Robert Cowan, grocer, tea and provision merchant, whose speciality was The Raiders blend of finest tea, 'entirely unique in character'. Beyond, on the same side, stands New Galloway's other hotel, the Cross Keys. The wealth of multi-storey buildings makes a mockery of the old 'one-storey' taunt.

Despite the hotel's name, the coat of arms on the facade of the Kenmure Arms seems to be that of the royal burgh; it was this which also appeared on the hotel notepaper. Below is the circular emblem of the Cyclists' Touring Club. In 1915 proprietor William Milligan promised moderate terms and every comfort, the white-starched maid at the door helping to provide the latter. C. H. Dick praised the Kenmure Arms for 'combining the excellences of the Dalry hotels'. The motor vehicle would provide the twice-daily connection with New Galloway station.

Many of the travellers on the Old Edinburgh Road who passed through New Galloway were pilgrims on their way to the shrine of St Ninian at Whithorn, the most important place of pilgrimage in Scotland before the Reformation. Their route crossed High Street at the town hall, and the West Port (illustrated here) formed the way from there to the edge of the burgh, after which the road continued to join the modern A712 at Achie cottage. The gradient and width of the West Port (port is Scots for 'gate') make it clear that wheeled vehicles were not expected. The latter could not have coped with the way across the moors to Minnigaff: travellers on foot and horseback frequently had difficulty negotiating this, especially the notorious Saddle Loup beside the Gray Mare's Tail.

West Port, New Galloway.

Wylie's Brae is one of the short streets running off High Street and Sunnyside (illustrated here) is at its foot. Its eastern exposure justifies its name. While its two-storey houses still stand, the cottages of Douglas Place, in the foreground, have been demolished and replaced by the local authority housing of Rosemount. Like numerous other houses in the burgh, the upper properties in Sunnyside are built of granite. Was this obtained from nearby Lowran (Bennan) Hill, or further afield? The carts in the middle ground suggest the proximity of a joiner's or carrier's business.

A troop of the Queen's Own Royal Glasgow Yeomanry approaches the north end of New Galloway's High Street watched at a respectful distance by an admiring crowd. Sadly the plumed coal-scuttle helmets of an earlier era had been dispensed with after the Boer War, except for ceremonial occasions. The regiment, a volunteer or territorial one, was formed in Glasgow in 1848 and soon became a prominent part of the city's social and civic life. It was probably in the New Galloway area on its annual camp, held in May. In addition to the Boer War, the Yeomanry fought in the First World War, two squadrons mounted until 1917 and the other two squadrons as cavalry throughout. In the Second World War they served, dismounted, as an anti-tank formation. The Stewartry had its own volunteer regiment, the Kirkcudbrightshire Gentlemen and Yeomanry Cavalry, which was raised about 1803 with a strength of 19 officers and 200 men. Its first colonel was Gordon of Greenlaw.

New Galloway's public park was the venue for the burgh's agricultural show, which was perhaps the oldest in Scotland. It started as a result of the existing weekly market and the formation of a farmers' club. As the picture illustrates, the show formerly had a big dairy cattle section, as almost every farm in Kells parish had a dairy. With changes in farming, Kells now has very few dairy farms and Blackfaced sheep form the biggest part of the show today. The traditional date of a Saturday at the end of September or beginning of October has been advanced to August, and the venue is now on the outskirts of the burgh on the way to Ken Bridge. The present event is called the Glenkens Show.

The steeple of the town hall is prominent in this view of New Galloway from the north-east. The four illuminated dials of its clock would certainly be visible to most of the community, justifying the efforts of Provost Milman and his fund-raisers in 1872. The tennis courts in the public park in the foreground have gone, to be replaced firstly by a bowling green, which was in operation in 1951, and then by the children's playground which occupies the site today.

21758. NEW GALLOWAY.   JUDGES' LTD

New Galloway and Black Craig.

The attractiveness of New Galloway's situation, with its houses sprinkled along the valley side between hills and loch, is best appreciated from the east. The River Ken, on the verge of becoming Loch Ken, can be glimpsed in the foreground while the background is dominated by Black Craig of Dee or Cairnsmore of Dee. To amend the popular local rhyme, this is 'the lowest of the three' Galloway Cairnsmores, overtopped by its lofty neighbour Cairnsmore of Carsphairn to the north and the rather less tall Cairnsmore of Fleet to the south-west.

Kells church overlooks New Galloway from the Ayr road to the north. Two hundred years ago its minister, the Revd John Gillespie, was head of a remarkable family. Two of his sons followed him into the ministry while they and their sister were accomplished local poets. William Gillespie, who succeeded his father in Kells, was involved in a local sensation in 1819. As chaplain to the local militia, the Kirkcudbrightshire Cavalry, he was asked to take the service in Kirkcudbright church during the regiment's annual camp. Disobeying a royal edict, he prayed for George IV's estranged wife, Caroline of Brunswick, and at the end of the service was placed under military arrest by the Cavalry's commander, a local laird. Although the act was largely symbolic, the minister complained to the Lord Advocate, and the CO was required to write a full apology.

New Galloway's celebrations of the formal ending of the Great War appear to be taking place on the golf course. Although this may seem strange, it is in fact entirely proper since the course is laid out on the 'town park' or common, that is the burgh land, on which all townspeople could collect fuel or graze animals. The common was therefore the appropriate location for a community event in a royal burgh.

GALLOWAY PEACE CELEBRATIONS 19th JULY 1919.

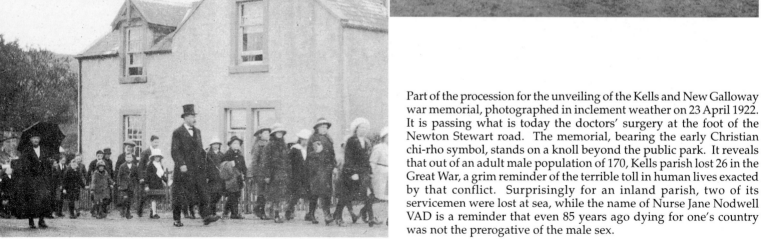

Part of the procession for the unveiling of the Kells and New Galloway war memorial, photographed in inclement weather on 23 April 1922. It is passing what is today the doctors' surgery at the foot of the Newton Stewart road. The memorial, bearing the early Christian chi-rho symbol, stands on a knoll beyond the public park. It reveals that out of an adult male population of 170, Kells parish lost 26 in the Great War, a grim reminder of the terrible toll in human lives exacted by that conflict. Surprisingly for an inland parish, two of its servicemen were lost at sea, while the name of Nurse Jane Nodwell VAD is a reminder that even 85 years ago dying for one's country was not the prerogative of the male sex.

The caption accompanying this photograph reads: 'New Galloway Carpet Bowling Team, Winners of Championship at Dumfries, 1st February, 1913.' The date of the photograph inevitably raises the question of whether the names of any of this group are inscribed on the local war memorial. New Galloway's carpet bowling club played in the building opposite the public park between the former school and the phone box. This appears in the right foreground of the picture on page 24. Now a private house but formerly a reading and recreation room, it housed the Industrial Section at the New Galloway Show.

Another recreational activity, but unlike carpet bowling one which is certainly not practised today. Two packs of otter hounds operated in the Glenkens. One was a private one, owned by prominent sportsman Captain Alexander Clark-Kennedy of Knockgray near Carsphairn, and known on every river in Dumfries and Galloway. The other was the Dumfriesshire Otter Hounds, founded in 1889 and still in existence in 1933. Like the other pack, it hunted in both Dumfries and Galloway. The reason that both packs operated over such a wide area stems from the distribution of otters: approximately one is found every five miles of water. The Balmaclellan minister's comment in 1840 that in the River Ken 'otters abound undisturbed' was destined to be contradicted.

OTTER HUNT ON THE KEN   NEW GALLOWAY

NEW GALLOWAY   GOLF CLUB   SUMMER MEETING

The hilly nature of the New Galloway golf course ensured that all prizes were well earned. Designed by Mr Baillie of Belfast, in 1951 it had a par of 68 and an amateur record of 65. At one time, because of the activities of rabbits, its fairways had something of the character of a seaside course. Visitors were warned 'caddies not always available'. In 1915 the Honorary Secretary was J. A. Courtenay of The Cottage, later to be provost of the burgh. Assistant Secretary was J. Mitchell, who at his premises in the High Street was agent for golf clubs and cycles and also a publisher of local postcard views. By 1937 Mr Mitchell was both postmaster and registrar.

Situated about twelve miles west of New Galloway overlooking the Newton Stewart road, Murray's Monument commemorates one of the most remarkable men Galloway has ever produced. Born in 1775, the son of the shepherd at nearby Dunkitterick, Alexander Murray was self-educated apart from brief spells at New Galloway and Minnigaff schools. Finding after three years as a shepherd that he was unable to follow his father's vocation because of poor eyesight, from the age of twelve he tutored the children of local farmers before obtaining a place and bursary at Edinburgh University at the age of seventeen. There he completed a divinity course, edited *The Scots Magazine*, and taught himself every language then known in Britain. After a spell as minister at Urr his genius for languages brought him the Professorship of Oriental Languages at his old university, but he died of tuberculosis in 1813 only a few months after his appointment. The assembly at Murray's Monument are marking the centenary of his death.

ALEXANDER MURRAY CENTENARY APRIL 16TH 1913

Only Murray's Monument and the bridge in the foreground provide evidence that this is indeed a scene on the New Galloway to Newton Stewart road opposite the former Forestry Commission caravan park. The house, outbuildings, and enclosures of Talnotry or Dunnottrie farm have disappeared without trace beneath a blanket of conifers. Of the entire area beyond the road only the triangular-shaped field in the middle foreground has not been smothered by trees. The A712 is of comparatively recent origin: until 200 years ago the highway (the Old Edinburgh Road) ran nearly half-a-mile to the north-west behind the hill crowned by the monument. When the new road was being built, a grim discovery was made near here: the skeleton and empty pack of a pedlar who had disappeared 50 years before. He had been robbed, murdered, and his body dumped in a spot seemingly too remote for discovery.

Ken Bridge, situated just east of New Galloway on the A712, was designed by John Rennie and built of local granite from Lowran Hill. It was completed in 1822 and replaced two earlier bridges, which had been washed away by the Ken in spate. The first of those was built around 1755. The number and size of the arches of the present bridge are presumably to prevent a recurrence of the previous mishaps by ensuring the unrestricted passage of water. To the same end the river bed was altered. A second reason for the large arches may have been the hope that the projected Glenkens canal would reach as far north as this. When the bridge was opened, Provost Murray of New Galloway (unrelated to the linguist) was officially invited to be first to cross. He managed to accomplish this in spite of the determined efforts of Viscount Kenmure – who was in the following carriage – to overtake him.

The former coaching inn at the east end of the Ken Bridge, now the Ken Bridge Hotel, here carries its earlier name of the Spalding Arms, the Spaldings having long been owners of the adjacent Holme estate outside Balmaclellan. Some kind of inn has almost definitely existed on the site for hundreds of years, for prior to the advent of a bridge travellers crossed the river in this vicinity by ferry or ford. The Spalding Arms could have been the venue for the dinner which Viscount Kenmure gave for fourteen of New Galloway's oldest residents to mark the opening of the 1822 bridge.

The Holme today is quite different from the building in the picture. The nineteenth century Tudor-style main block of the house, on the right, was demolished 30 years ago and the single-storey wings, one of which is visible on the left, were converted into a new house. Almost inevitably the estate was owned at one time by a branch of the Gordon family before being bought by the first Spalding owner in 1751. The Spaldings were an adventurous family. Two hundred years ago one of them fought a duel with Viscount Kenmure at Kirkcudbright, while another Spalding was killed in the Crimean War serving with the Naval Brigade at Sebastopol.

As Troquhain (right) lies on the other side of Balmaclellan from Holme, its inclusion in a book on the Ken valley will raise eyebrows. However, in the nineteenth century it was owned by the redoubtable Provost Murray of New Galloway, being one of four local estates which his success in business allowed him to purchase. Among its owners in earlier times were the Griersons of Lag, destined to become the arch-foes of the Covenanters, and, unsurprisingly, the Gordons of Lochinvar. Its most exotic proprietor, in the late eighteenth century, was one Perlas Mounsey, physician extraordinary to Empress Catherine of Russia.

Airds House, a mile north of Parton on the Ayr road, dates from the late nineteenth century and for most of its existence has been the home of the Henniker-Hughan family, one of whom was MP for Galloway in the 1920s. This is one of four examples of the place name Airds in the vicinity. Further afield it is found in three other Stewartry parishes with several examples just east of Stranraer. The Wigtownshire form 'Aird' (high place) is true to the original Gaelic while in the Stewartry the final 's' was added when the name was anglicised. The meaning 'high place' seems in some cases to have been used relatively, indicating a location close to low-lying land by the river or coast, and just high enough to avoid the risk of flooding.

This picture shows two different means of crossing Loch Ken with the older ferry, which gave Boat of Rhone its name, in the shadow of the railway viaduct, one of the main civil engineering works on the Dumfries to Stranraer line. A request by the Stewartry roads authority to incorporate a road bridge in the viaduct was rejected by the railway company because of a perceived risk to road users. However, it was rail users who were at risk in December 1935, when the Stranraer-bound 'Paddy' was derailed in the early morning at the west end of the viaduct. The two engines stayed upright but the seven coaches went down the embankment. Fortunately no one was seriously injured, the main damage being sustained by a postal sorting van, which was smashed to pieces. The viaduct, still standing today, has been much admired for its design.

The Boat of Rhone is probably the best known ferry crossing on the Ken. An 1896 writer records that the ferry was rarely used at that time, but it was still in operation in 1916. The crossing provides the basis of the plot in S. R. Crockett's short story *A Cry Across the Black Water*, the cry being the summons of an intending passenger to the ferryperson's cottage on the opposite bank. Crockett's tale narrates the ill-fated love between ferrygirl Grace Allen and aristocratic Gregory Jeffray, youthful sheriff of the Stewartry on the fast track to political/legal advancement. Crockett relocates Shakespeare's tragic tale of Hamlet and Ophelia to the shores of Loch Ken but with a different ending. With typical Galloway sturdiness of character, Grace returns from beyond the grave to exact watery revenge on her faithless lover.

"Parton from Station House."

Hemmed in between road and loch, the railway ran close to the former at Parton. Today almost nothing remains of the stationmaster's house at the north end of the village. Careful examination reveals a scatter of rubble in the belt of conifers screening the new housing development on the west side of the road, which is built on the site of the old goods yard. The bridge helps to identify the location. In 1907 the goods yard was where George Bryson, mineral agent, Parton station, conducted his business, selling coal, lime and bricks. By 1915 he had relocated to nearby Boreland of Parton. North of the goods yard was the station itself, also close to the road and now a private house.

Of Parton, Pigot's *Commercial Directory* for 1826 states: 'The village contains about a dozen houses; the only one worthy of notice is the manse'. Things changed radically after Benjamin Rigby Murray, a Manchester manufacturer related to the Murrays of Troquhain, bought the estate in 1852. In 1901 he rebuilt the estate village, transforming it into a model of its kind. As well as the dormer windows and ornamental porches visible here, the houses had hanging lamps in each doorway. A notable feature was the community building in the foreground with its wooden clock tower, which served either as reading room or laundry (accounts vary). Not visible but tucked discreetly away behind the houses is another community amenity, the famous Parton Privy, an elegant, octagonal, brick structure with eight compartments.

At the south end of Parton a wall plaque (visible here) commemorates Rigby Murray, describing his rebuilding of the village as 'the last act of a kindly life'. The fountain in the right foreground, as its inscription declares, was erected by local people 'in grateful remembrance of their friend B. Rigby Murray'. Another plaque on a nearby house brings the Parton story up to date. It is dated 1979 and pays tribute to builder William Gibson of Barnbarroch, whose reconstruction work on the village saved it from destruction. The privy has also been restored and converted to a summer house, with one compartment retained in its original form. However, B. Rigby Murray's munificence could not safeguard Parton from the risk of flooding from nearby Loch Ken. An eighteenth century writer declared that the loch at this point could rise eight feet in a spate, and a photo from around 1900 in the Stewartry Museum shows the waters perilously close to Parton.

Most of Parton's public buildings present themselves for inspection in this portmanteau shot: the old school house and old and new churches. Least conspicuous and peeping coyly from the trees on the left is the bell tower of the parish church, reputedly built in 1592. The 1792 incumbent remarked sadly that it was 'remarkable for little else than its darkness and disproportion'. Today the remains are a burial enclosure, housing the grave of local man James Clerk Maxwell, a physicist of towering genius ranked alongside Newton and Einstein. The old schoolhouse (centre) contained both schoolroom and, belatedly, schoolmaster's residence. It was rebuilt several times on the same site with remarkable economy, the 1795 version costing £61. By 1861 the building was declared uninhabitable and school was held in the church until a new structure could be built. The modern, nineteenth century church on the right contains a sixteenth century carved stone slab.

Set some distance back from the road at the foot of a wooded hill and described by a nineteenth century writer as 'delightfully situated', the manse – at this period with tennis court – reflects an atmosphere of gracious living that would perhaps have left the spirits of local Covenanters a trifle uneasy. With electricity installed just before the Second World War through the generosity of a member of the congregation, it was large enough to accommodate meetings of various church organisations in the 1960s. But big, as is well known, is not always beautiful: the minister of that time commented ruefully on the expense of maintaining the extensive grounds.

Prior to the arrival of the Rigby Murrays in the mid-nineteenth century, Parton estate had been owned for 400 years by the Glendonwyn family. In a break from the normal Galloway pattern, a Glendonwyn forfeited the estate in the seventeenth century not for his support of the Presbyterian cause but for his following the Marquis of Montrose in the cause of Charles I. The lands were later regained. With the exception of one wing, the fire-damaged nineteenth century Parton House was demolished in 1966 by the new owner of the estate, Edward Hunter-Blair (now Sir Edward), and replaced by a two-storey Colt cedar building.

Crossmichael, known in early times as Corsemichael, derives its name from a cross dedicated to St Michael which is assumed to have stood on the site of the present village, although no trace or tradition of its exact site survives. This is despite the fact that an annual fair held beside the cross in late September or October continued until the mid-nineteenth century. Equally unknown is the site of the fight close by at Spearford between the Glendonwyns of Parton and the Gordons of Kenmure, a conflict celebrated by local poet Samuel Wilson in *The Battle of Spearford*. Whether fair or fight is attracting the crowd in this view of the village main street from the north is not known.

From the south the parish church stands out prominently. It was built in 1751 and enlarged before the end of the century, although the unusual, small, rounded spire is probably much older, dating to the early seventeenth century. The church's eccentric eighteenth century minister, Nathaniel M'Kie, punctuated his scripture readings with admonitions to his flock, frequently to their confusion: ' "And the Lord said unto Moses" – sneck that door; I'm thinkin if ye had to sit beside the door yersel ye wadnae be sae ready tae leave it open'! A number of interesting headstones in the churchyard includes one to Covenanter William Graham, summarily executed by Claverhouse's dragoons in 1682.

R. Nisbet's premises (beyond the road junction in the right middleground) have long gone, to be replaced by a modern bungalow, but the Thistle Inn, boldly advertising its name on its chimney, remains, a thoroughly respectable successor to the 'dram-houses' complained of by the minister in 1791. People were apparently tempted to frequent those too much because of their abundant supplies of cheap, smuggled whisky. As with the rest of Galloway the population and prosperity of Crossmichael peaked in the mid-nineteenth century, when the village had three schools, four shopkeepers, four joiners, two vintners, two shoemakers, a clogmaker, a blacksmith, a tailor, and a miller; more unusual trades were those of letter cutter and well sinker. This contrasted with 1826 when the only representatives of trade and commerce were two grocers and three publicans; unexpectedly one of the latter was also a joiner.

The stooks of corn in the foreground reveal that this is a scene from the past, although the presence of the local authority houses of Old Ferry Road on the left proves the picture was not taken before the late 1930s. In this more recent past, the parish church (centre background) was occupied by a locally famous name, that of Revd J. A. Fisher, Convener of Stewartry County Council in the post-war years. An embodiment of the church militant, he was wounded as a combatant soldier in the First World War and in the Second served as a Home Guard battalion commander, frequently preaching on a Sunday wearing battle dress under his ministerial robes. The story of this remarkable man can be found in his daughter's autobiography, *My Father's House*.

RIVER DEE FROM CROSSMICHAEL STATION. (1)

The raising of the level of the Ken by the hydroelectric scheme of 1936 brought Crossmichael station alarmingly close to the loch's waters. In her biography, Pauline Neville, née Fisher, records how the boat train, the legendary 'Paddy', nightly made a 'surprising and dramatic halt at our little station'. The close proximity of station to village had regrettable results in June 1873 when three of the four crew of the Stranraer-bound goods train adjourned for refreshment to a local hostelry before resuming their journey. Thus fortified they continued briskly on their way and at Creetown ran through two red signals into the rear of a waiting passenger train. Fortunately no serious injuries were sustained but their employment was brought to a termination.